ISBN: 0-89898-473-4

SONGS YOU KNOW BY HEART
JIMMY BUFFETT'S GREATEST HIT(S)

© 1991 CPP/Belwin, Inc.
15800 N.W. 48th Avenue, Miami, Florida 33014

Album Cover Art: © 1985 MCA Records, Inc.
Color Photography: Jim Shea
Text Photography: Henry Diltz
Transcriptions: Aaron Stang
Editor: Carol Cuellar

BOAT DRINKS . . . 14
CHANGES IN LATITUDES,
CHANGES IN ATTITUDES . . . 20
CHEESEBURGER IN PARADISE . . . 24
COME MONDAY . . . 7
FINS . . . 30
GRAPEFRUIT-JUICY FRUIT . . . 40
HE WENT TO PARIS . . . 50
MARGARITAVILLE . . . 10
PENCIL THIN MUSTACHE . . . 45
A PIRATE LOOKS AT FORTY . . . 58
SON OF A SON OF A SAILOR . . . 63
VOLCANO . . . 72
WHY DON'T WE GET DRUNK . . . 76

COME MONDAY

Words and Music by
JIMMY BUFFETT

Come Monday-3-1

8

Chorus:

Mon - day _____ it'll be all right. __ Come Mon - day _____ I'll be

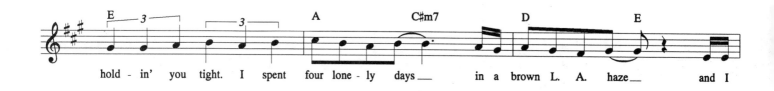

hold - in' you tight. I spent four lone - ly days __ in a brown L. A. haze __ and I

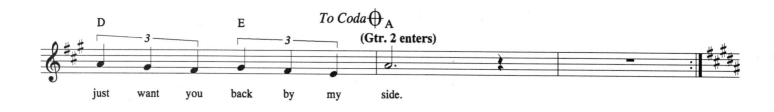

just want you back by my side.

I can't help it hon - ey, you're that much a part __

_____ of me now. __ Re - mem - ber that night __

_____ in Mon - tan - a when we said there'd be no room for

doubt?

Pedal steel arr. for gtr.

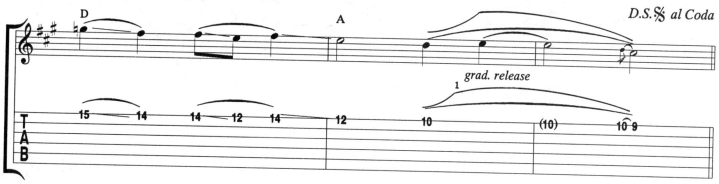

D.S. ℅ al Coda

grad. release

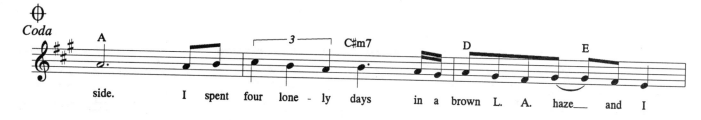

Coda

side.　I　spent　four　lone - ly　days　in　a　brown　L. A.　haze___　and　I

just　want　you　back　by　my　side. _____

Verse 2.

Yes, it's been quite a summer,
Rent-a-cars and West bound trains,
And now you're off on vacation,
Somethin' you tried to explain.
And darlin' it's I love you so,
That's the reason I just let you go.

(To Chorus:)

Verse 3.

I hope you're enjoyin' the scen'ry,
I know that it's pretty up there.
We can go hikin' on Tuesday,
With you I'd walk anywhere.
California has worn me quite thin,
I just can't wait to see you again.

(To Chorus:)

MARGARITAVILLE

Words and Music by
JIMMY BUFFETT

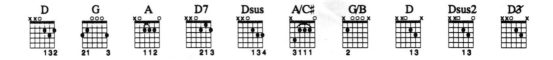

Moderately ♩ = 116

Flute and keyboard arr. for guitar

Verses 1, 2 & 3:

1. Nib - blin' on _ sponge - cake,   watch-in' the sun
2. Don't know the rea - son,   I stayed here all sea-
3. *See additional lyrics.*

_ bake;   all of those tour - ists   cov - ered with oil. _
- son   with noth - ing to show _ but this   brand - new tat - too. _

(cont. strumming simile)

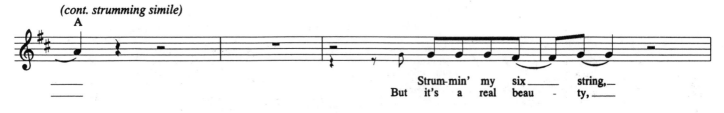

_   Strum-min' my six _ string, _
_   But it's a real beau - ty, _

Margaritaville-4-1

on my front porch___ swing.___ Smell those shrimp;___
a Mex - i - can cu - tie, ___ how it got here ___

___ they're be - gin - ning to boil.
___ I have - n't a clue.___

Chorus:

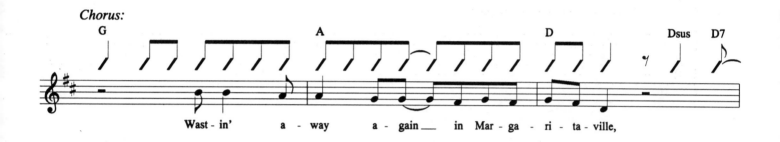

Wast - in' a - way a - gain ___ in Mar - ga - ri - ta - ville,

search - in' for my _____ lost sha - ker of salt.___

___ Some ___ peo - ple claim___

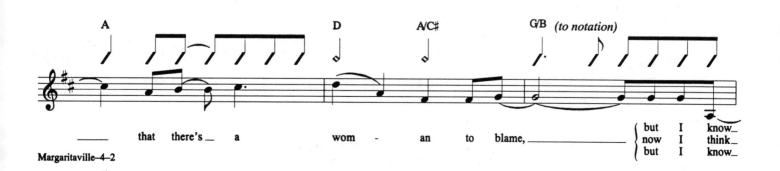

___ that there's ___ a wom - an to blame, _____
but I know___
now I think___
but I know___

Margaritaville-4-2

it's no - bod- y's fault. ___
hell, it could ___ be my fault. ___
it's my own ___ damn ___ fault. ___

Margaritaville–4–3

Verse 3:

I blew out my flip-flop,
Stepped on a pop top;
Cut my heel, had to cruise on back home.
But there's booze in the blender,
And soon it will render
That frozen concoction that helps me hang on.

Margaritaville-4-4

BOAT DRINKS

Words and Music by
JIMMY BUFFETT

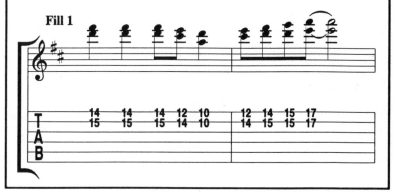

To Coda

Twen - ty de - grees___ and the hock-

I'm close to bod - i - ly harm.
I got - ta go where it's

(Elec. Gtr. 2)

- ey game's on.

No - bod - y cares; they are way___ too far gone,___ scream - in', "Boat

Elec. Gtr. 1

8va

___ drinks,"

some - thin' to keep___ 'em all warm.

8va

*Slide Gtr.

Elec. Gtr. 2

*Tab #'s for slide gtr. are in italics

This morn - in'

I shot six holes in my

18

Boat Drinks—6–5

CHANGES IN LATITUDES, CHANGES IN ATTITUDES

Words and Music by
JIMMY BUFFETT

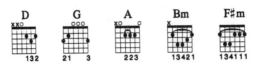

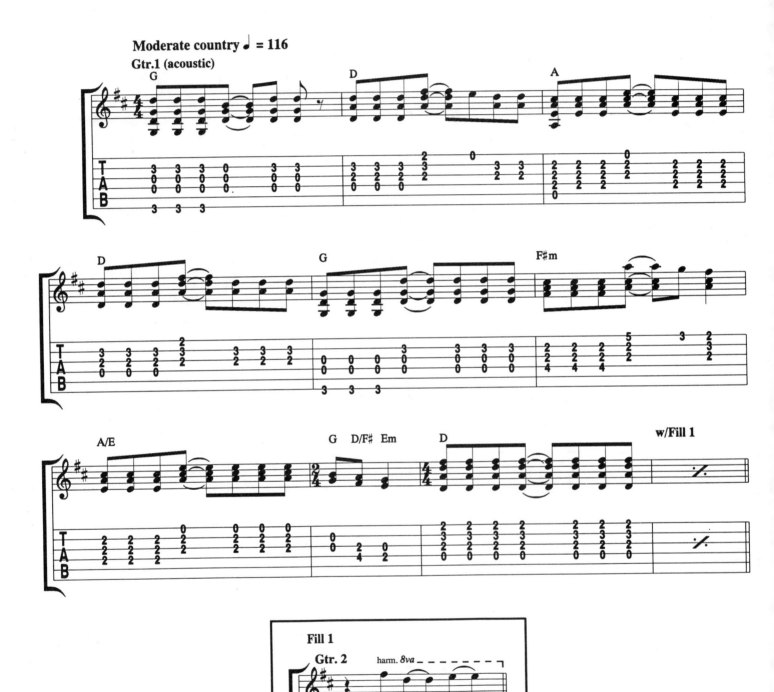

Changes In Latitudes, Changes In Attitudes—4-1

Changes In Latitudes, Changes in Attitudes—4–2

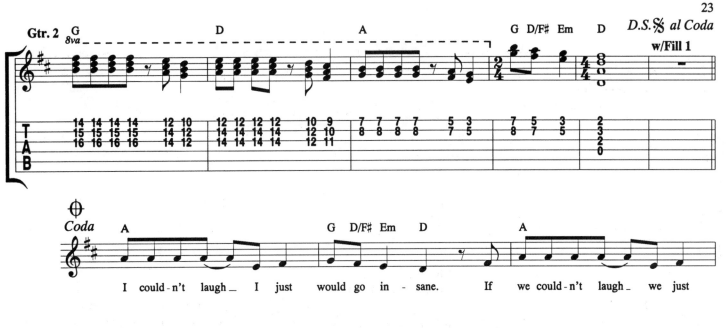

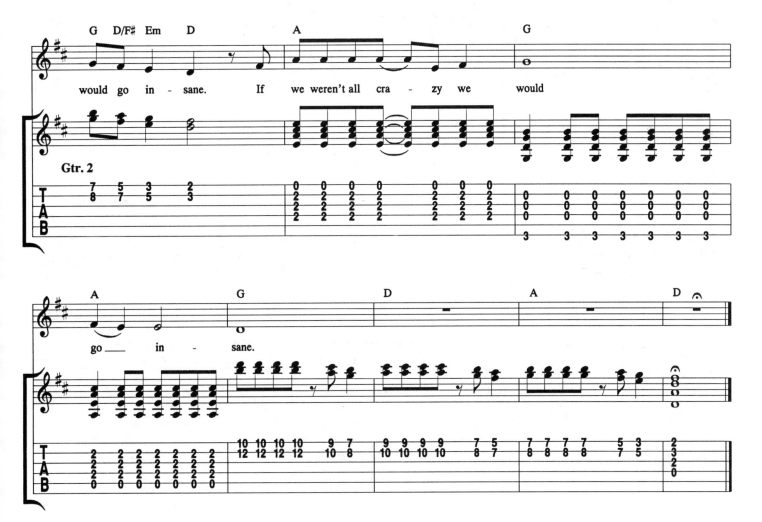

Verse 3:

I think about Paris when I'm on high red wine;
I wish I could jump on a plane.
And so many nights I just dream of the ocean.
God, I wish I was sailing again.
Oh, yesterdays are over my shoulder,
So I can't look back for too long.
There's just too much to see waiting in front of me,
And I know that I just can't go wrong. With these. . .
(To Chorus:)

CHEESEBURGER IN PARADISE

Words and Music by
JIMMY BUFFETT

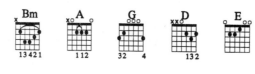

Bright beat ♩ = 138

Tried to a - mend

Verse:

——— my car - niv - o - rous hab - its. Made it near - ly sev - en - ty days,__

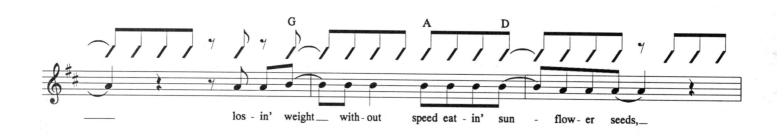

——— los - in' weight__ with - out speed eat - in' sun - flow - er seeds,__

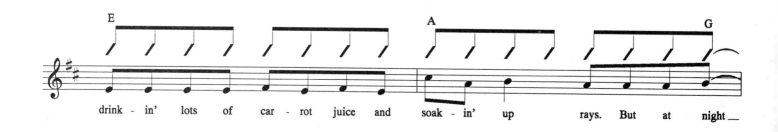

drink - in' lots of car - rot juice and soak - in' up rays. But at night __

Cheeseburger in Paradise–6–1

26

Cheeseburger in Paradise—6–3

* Tune ③ to G♯ for Slide Gtr.

Cheeseburger in Paradise–6–4

Chorus:
(Rhy. Gtr. same as previous Verse and Chorus)

cheese - bur - ger in par - a - dise?___ Mak - in' the best ___ of ev - 'ry

vir - tue and vice. _____ Worth ev - 'ry damn _____ bit of

sac - ri - fice _____ to get a cheese - bur - ger in

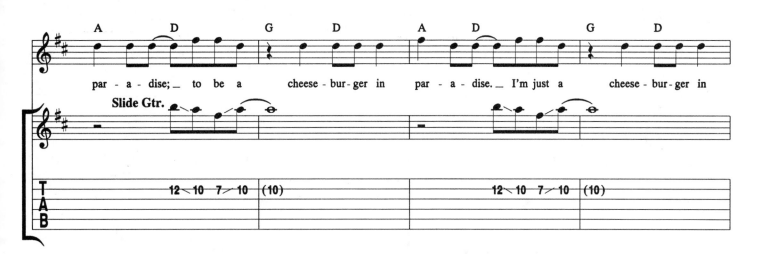

par - a - dise; __ to be a cheese - bur - ger in par - a - dise. __ I'm just a cheese - bur - ger in

Slide Gtr.

TAB: 12~10 7~10 (10)   12~10 7~10 (10)

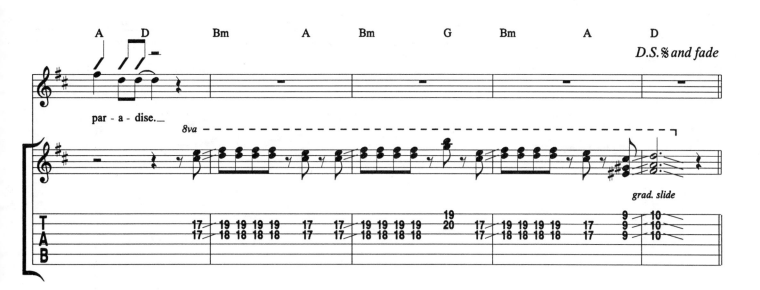

par - a - dise. __

D.S. % and fade

8va ------

grad. slide

FINS

Words and Music by
JIMMY BUFFETT, DEBORAH McCOLL,
BARRY CHANCE and TOM CORCORAN

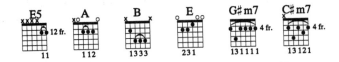

Fins–10–1

She came down __

from Cin - cin - nat - i.   It took her three days   on   the train.

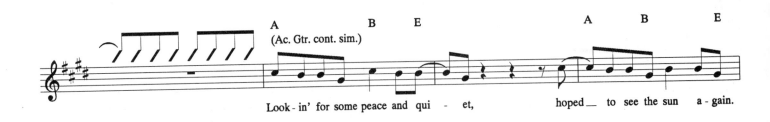

Look - in' for some peace and qui - et,   hoped __ to see the sun a - gain.

But now she lives down by the o - cean.   She's tak - in'

care   to look   for sharks.   They hang out   in   the lo -

* Tab #'s for Gtr. 2 are printed in italics.

Verse 2:
(Ac. Gtr. same as Verse 1)

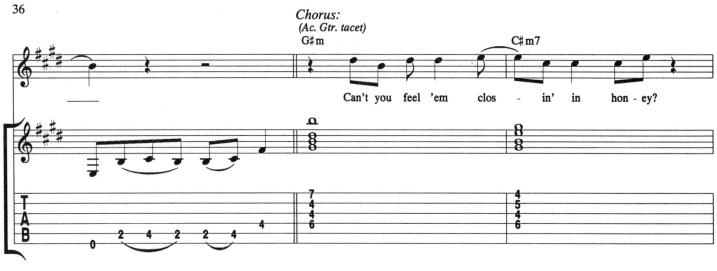

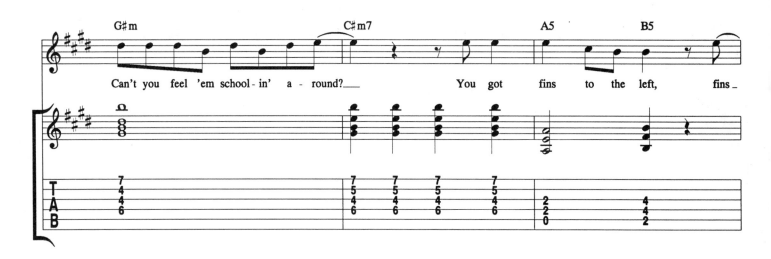

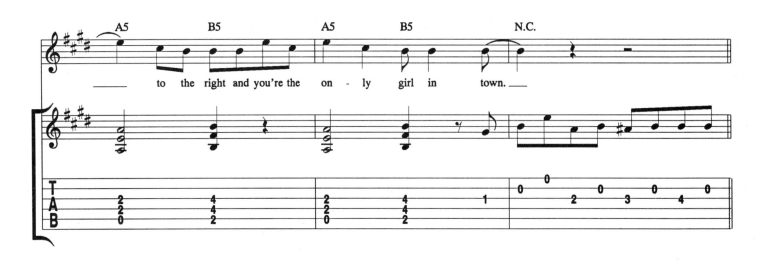

GRAPEFRUIT-JUICY FRUIT

Words and Music by
JIMMY BUFFETT

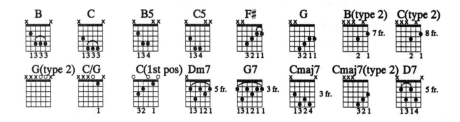

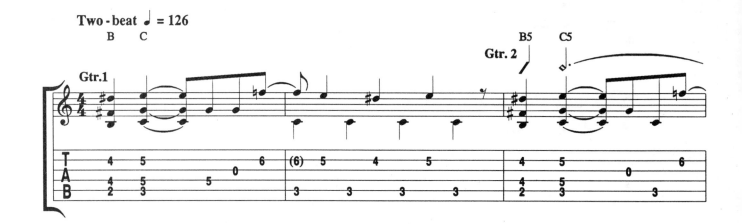

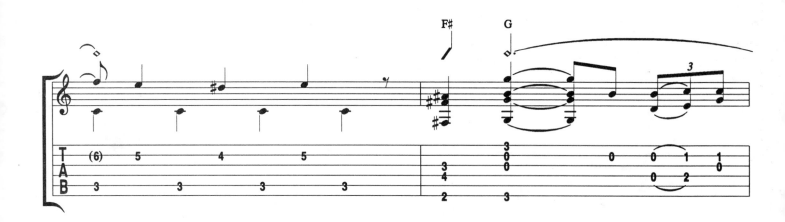

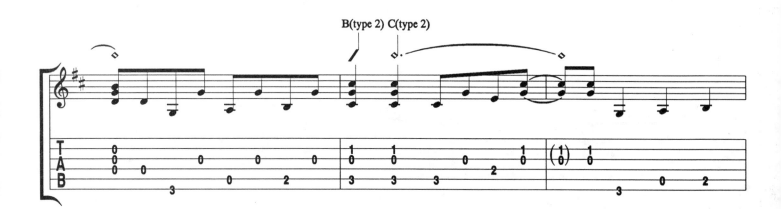

Grapefruit-Juicy Fruit–5–1

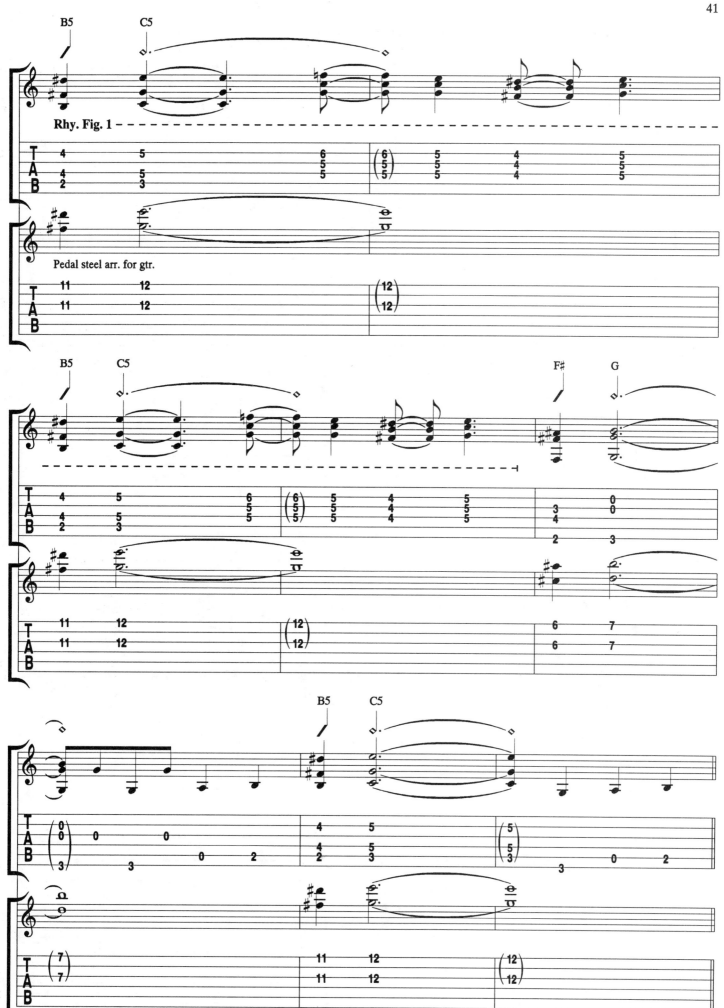

Grapefruit-Juicy Fruit-5-2

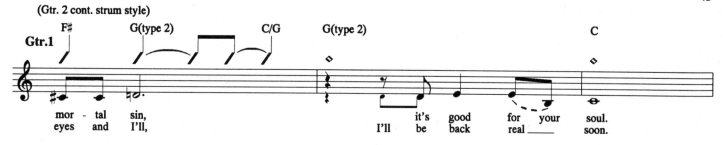

(Gtr. 2 cont. strum style)

Gtr.1

F# G(type 2) C/G G(type 2) C

mor - tal sin, it's good for your soul.
eyes and I'll, I'll be back real ___ soon.

Chorus:

Dm7 G7

1. Ya know it ___ gets
2. *(Instrumental)*

Cmaj7 Dm7 G7

so damn lone - ly ___ when you're __

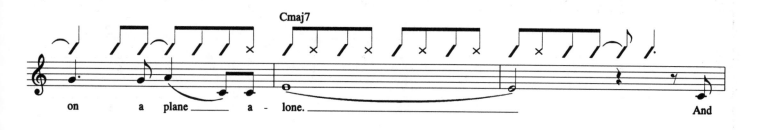

Cmaj7

on a plane __ a - lone. ___ And

Dm7 *(sim.)* G7 Cmaj7(type 2)

if I had the mon - ey, hon - ey, I'd strap you in be - side __

Grapefruit-Juicy Fruit–5–4

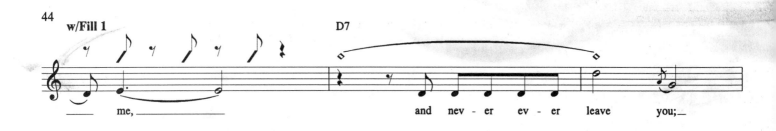

w/Fill 1

D7

— me, — — — and nev - er ev - er leave you; —

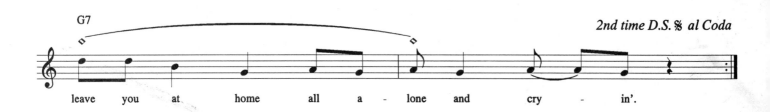

G7

2nd time D.S. ℅ al Coda

leave you at home all a - lone and cry - in'.

Coda

C

F♯   G

night.   Yeah, ya chew a lit - tle Juic - y Fruit,

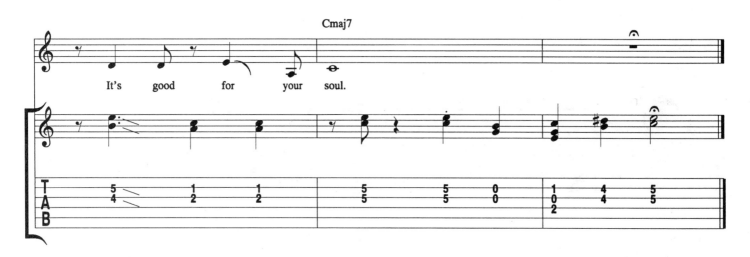

Cmaj7

It's good for your soul.

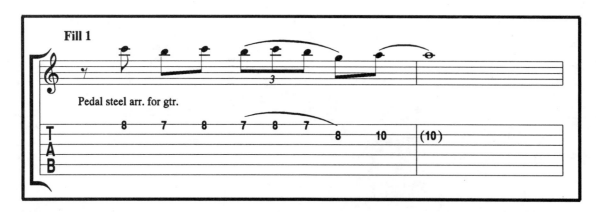

Fill 1

Pedal steel arr. for gtr.

PENCIL THIN MUSTACHE

Words and Music by
JIMMY BUFFETT

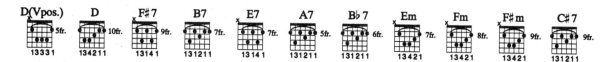

Intro:
Gtr. 1 cont. simile
Verse :

Now they make new mov-ies in old black and white, ___

Pencil Thin Mustache–5–1

46

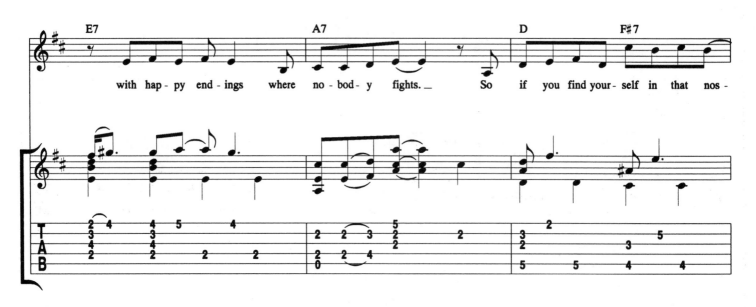

Pencil Thin Mustache–5–2

Chorus:
Gtrs. 1 & 2

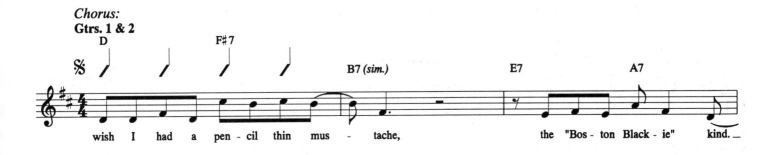

wish I had a pen - cil thin mus - tache, the "Bos - ton Black - ie" kind. __

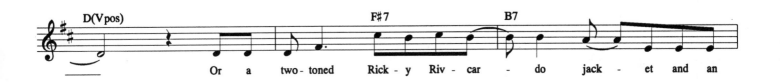

Or a two - toned Rick - y Riv - car - do jack - et and an

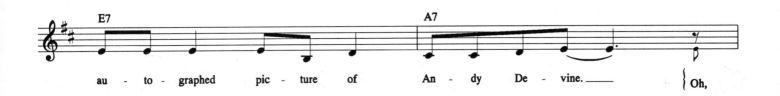

au - to - graphed pic - ture of An - dy De - vine. ___ { Oh,

I re - mem - ber be - in' buck - toothed and skin - ny; writ - ing fan let - ters to Sky's
I could be an - y - one I want - ed to be, may - be suave Er - rol Flynn or the Sheik

__ niece, Pen - ny. Oh, I wish I had a pen - cil - thin mus -
__ of Ar - a - by. If I on - ly had a pen - cil - thin mus -

To Coda

- tache, then I could solve some mys - t'ries too. Oh, it's
- tache, then I could do some cruis - ing too. Yeah,

Pencil Thin Mustache–5–3

Verse:

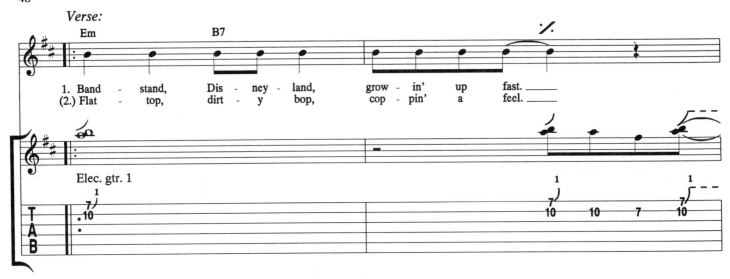

1. Band - stand, Dis - ney - land, grow - in' up fast. _____
(2.) Flat - top, dirt - y bop, cop - in' a feel. _____

Elec. gtr. 1

Drink - in' on a fake I. _____ D.; _____ Yeah,
Grub - in' on the liv - in' room floor. _____ They

Ra - ma of the jun - gle was ev - 'ry one's Ba - wan - na, and
send you off to col - lege, try to gain a lit - tle know - ledge, but

on - ly jazz mu - si - cians were smok - in' mar - i - jua - na. Yeah, wish I had a pen - cil - thin mus -
all you want to do is

- tache, then I could solve some mys - t'ries too.

Pencil Thin Mustache—5—4

HE WENT TO PARIS

Words and Music by
JIMMY BUFFETT

*Let all notes ring.

*Gtr. 2 is capoed at the 7th fret. Any note
played at the 7th fret is played as an open string.

*Tab #'s for gtr. 3 are in italics.

He Went To Paris—8–1

52

He Went To Paris—8–3

He Went To Paris—8–4

Verse 2:

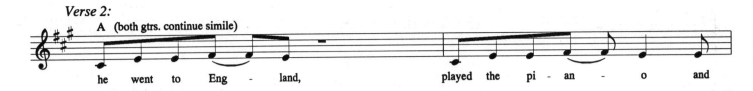

he went to Eng - land, played the pi - an - o and

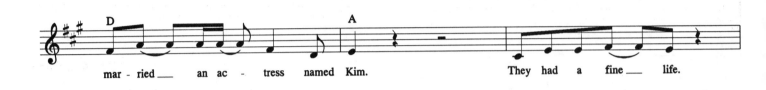

mar - ried ___ an ac - tress named Kim. They had a fine ___ life.

She was a good wife and bore him a young ___ son named Jim.

And all of the an - swers and all of the ques - tions

locked in his at - tic one day. 'Cause

he liked the qui - et clean coun - try liv - in' and twen - ty more years ___ slipped a -

He Went To Paris—8–5

*Tab #'s for gtr. 2 are in italics.

He Went To Paris—8–6

He Went To Paris–8–8

A PIRATE LOOKS AT FORTY

Words and Music by
JIMMY BUFFETT

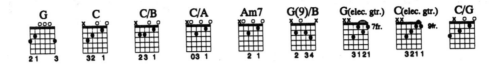

Moderate ♩ = 100
Intro:
Acoustic Gtr.

*Let all chords ring.

A Pirate Looks at Forty—5–1

Acoustic gtr. same as verse 1
Elec. Gtr. (1st time only)

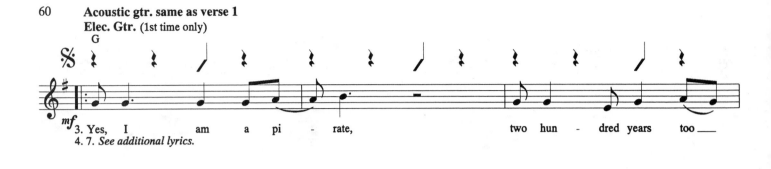

mf
3. Yes, I am a pi - rate, two hun - dred years too ___ late.
4. 7. *See additional lyrics.*

The can - nons don't thun - der, there's noth - in' to plun - der, I'm an

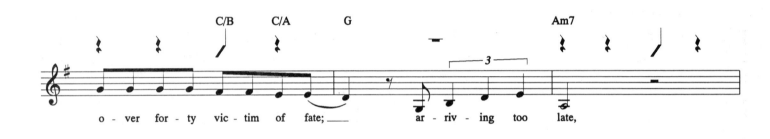

o - ver for - ty vic - tim of fate; ___ ar - riv - ing too late,

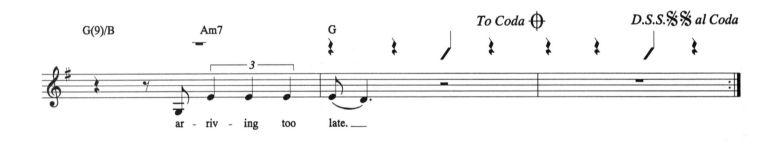

ar - riv - ing too late. ___

Acoustic gtr. same as other verses

5. I have been drunk ___ now for o - ver two weeks, I passed out and I ral - lied and I

sprung a few leaks, but I've got to stop wish - in', got to go fish - in', I'm down ___

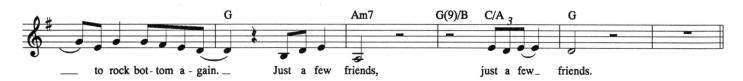

to rock bot - tom a - gain. Just a few friends, just a few_ friends.

Gtr. solo:
Acoustic gtr. continue simile

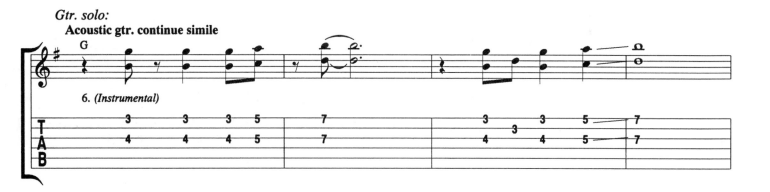

6. *(Instrumental)*

Marimba arr. for gtr. *Piano arr. for gtr.*

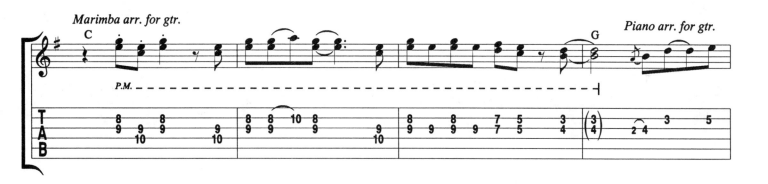

P.M.

D.S. 𝄋

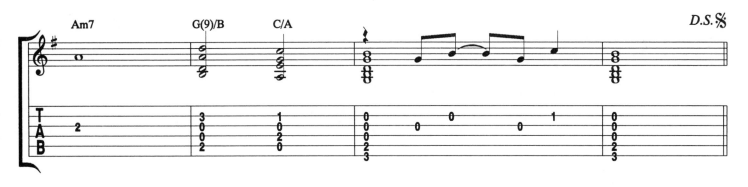

Coda

I feel like I've drowned, gon - na head up

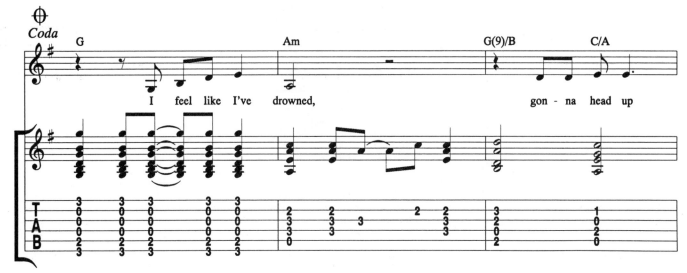

town.

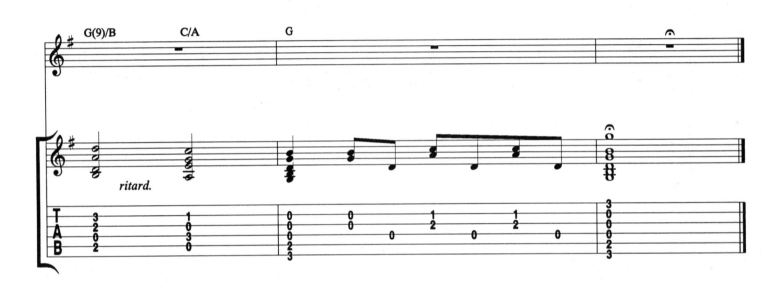

ritard.

Verse 2:

Watched the men who rode you,
Switch from sails to steam.
And in your belly you hold the treasure
That few have ever seen. Most of them dreams,
Most of them dreams.

Verse 4:

I've done a bit of smugglin'.
I've run my share of grass.
I made enough money to buy Miami,
But I pissed it away so fast. Never meant to last,
Never meant to last.

Verse 6:
(Instrumental)

Verse 7:

I go for younger women,
Lived with several awhile,
And though I ran away, they'll come back one day,
And still I can manage a smile.
It just takes awhile, just takes awhile.

Verse 8:

Mother, mother ocean, after all these years I've found
My occupational hazard being my occupation's just not around.
I feel like I've drowned,
Gonna head uptown.

SON OF A SON OF A SAILOR

Words and Music by
JIMMY BUFFETT

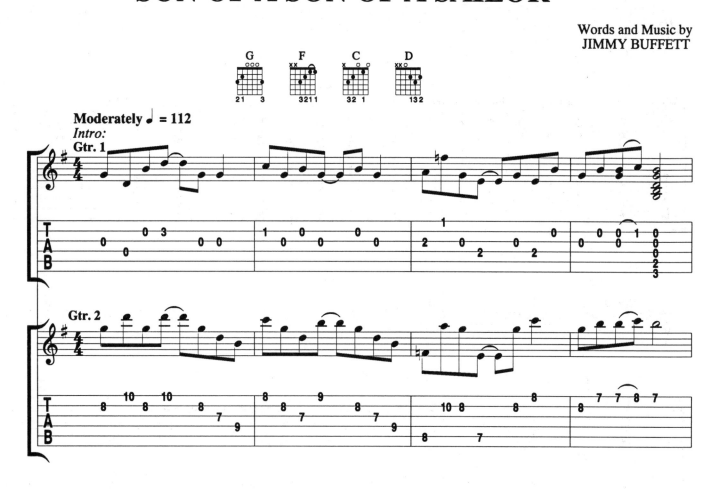

Son of a Son of a Sailor—9–1

Verse:

1. son of a son ___ of a sail - or, I ___ went

3. 4. *See additional lyrics.*

out on the sea ___ for ad - ven - ture; ex -

Son of a Son of a Sailor–9–2

Verse 2:
Gtrs. 1 & 2 cont. simile

dream - er of dreams ___ and a trav - el - in' man, ___ I have

chalked up man - y a mile. ___ Read doz - ens of books ___ a - bout

he - roes and crooks ___ and I've learned ___ much from both of their styles.

Chorus:
Gtr. 2 tacet 4 bars

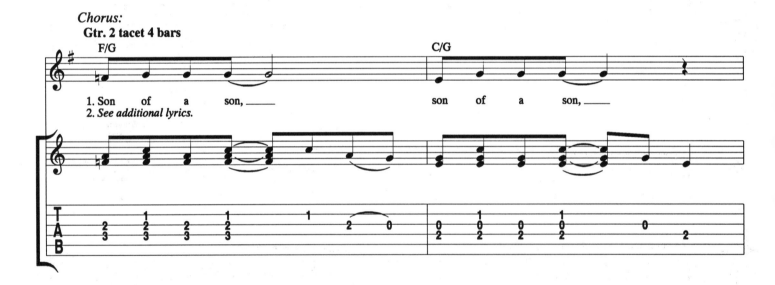

1. Son of a son, ___ son of a son, ___
2. *See additional lyrics.*

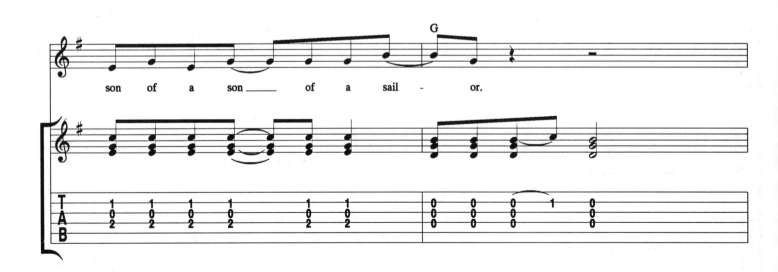

son of a son ___ of a sail - or.

Son of a Son of a Sailor–9–4

Son of a Son of a Sailor–9–5

68

Interlude:

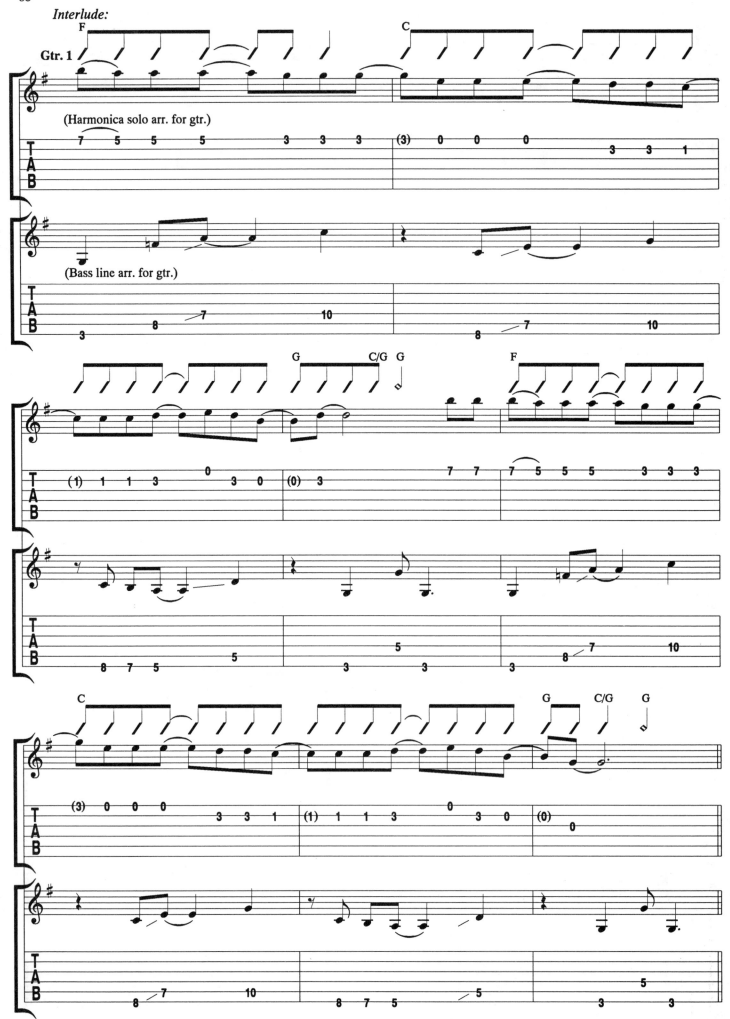

(Harmonica solo arr. for gtr.)

(Bass line arr. for gtr.)

Son of a Son of a Sailor–9–6

Son of a Son of a Sailor–9–7

70

Son of a Son of a Sailor–9–8

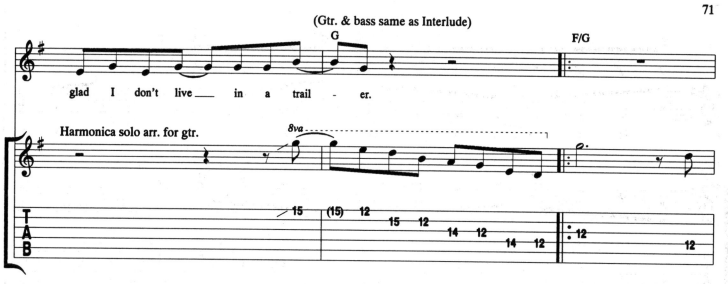

Verses 3 & 4:

Now away in the near future,
South-east of disorder,
You can shake the hand of the mango man
As he greets you at the border.
And the lady she hails from Trinidad;
Island of the spices.
Salt for your meat, and cinnamon sweet,
And the rum is for all your good vices.

Chorus 2:

Haul the sheet in as we ride on the wind
That our fore-fathers harnessed before us.
Hear the bells ring as the tide rigging sings.
It's a son of a gun of a chorus.

VOLCANO

Words and Music by
**JIMMY BUFFETT,
KEITH SYKES** and
HARRY DAILEY

*Consider Rhy. Figs. 1 & 2A models for improvisation.

Volcano–4–1

Verses 1, 2 & 3
*Rhy. Fig.1

1. Ground, she's mov - in' un - der me.
2. My girl ___ quick - ly said to me,
3. *See additional lyrics.*

Ti - dal waves ___ out on the sea.
"Mon, you bet - ter watch your feet.

Sul - phur smoke ___ up in the sky.
La - va come ___ down soft and hot.

You bet - ter

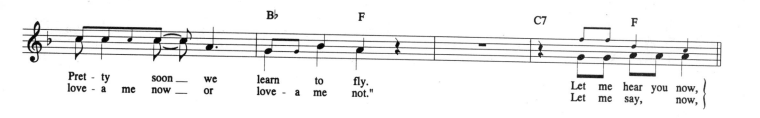

Pret - ty soon ___ we learn to fly.
love - a me now ___ or love - a me not."

Let me hear you now,
Let me say, now,

Chorus:
*w/Rhy. Fig. 2A

I don't ___ know, I don't ___ know, I don't know ___ where I'm ___

- a - gon - na go when the vol - ca - no blow. Now, Mis - ter Ut - tly!

Volcano–4–2

Instrumental:
(w/Rhy. Fig.2)

(Piano & steel drum)

Chorus:
w/Rhy. Fig. 2A

One more now, I don't __ know I don't __ know,

To Coda

I don't know __ where I'm - a - gon-na go when the vol - ca - no blow. But, I

Verses 4, 5 & 6:
w/Rhy. Fig. 2A

4. don't want to land __ in New York Cit - y, I don't want to land __ in
5. don't want to land __ in Com-man - che Sky Park, or in __ Nash - ville,
6. *See additional lyrics.*

Mex - i - co. I don't want to land __ on no Three Mile Is - land; I
Ten - nes - see. I don't want to land __ in no San Juan air - port

don't want to see ___ my skin a - glow. ___ more to say.
or the Yu - kon ter - ri - tor - y. ___

D.S. 𝄋 al Coda

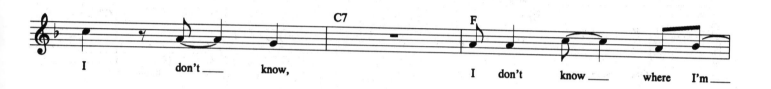

Coda

w/Rhy. Fig. 2A
F

Just - a one more. I don't ___ know,

C7   F

I don't ___ know, I don't know ___ where I'm ___

B♭   F   C7   F

___ a - gon - na go when the vol - ca - no blow.

Verse 3:

No time to count what I'm worth,
'Cause I just left the planet Earth.
Where I go I hope there's rum.
Not to worry, mon soon come.

Verse 6:

Don't want to land no San Diego.
Don't want to land in no Buzzard's Bay.
I don't want to land on no Ayatollah.
I got nothin' more to say.

WHY DON'T WE GET DRUNK

Words and Music by
M. GARDENS

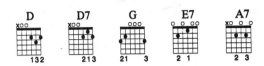

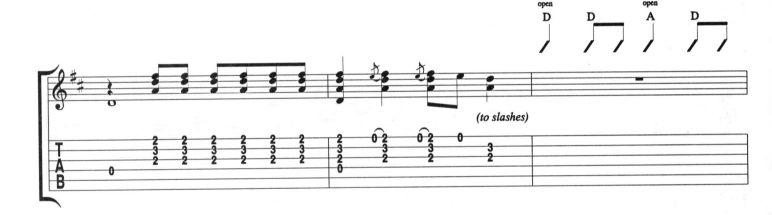

Why Don't We Get Drunk–3–1

Chorus: G — D — Gtr.1 — sim.

Why don't we get drunk and screw?

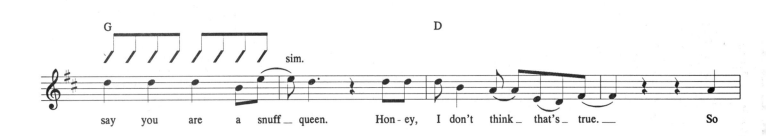

E7 — A7

I just bought a wa-ter bed, it's filled up for me and you. They

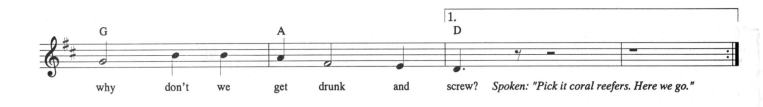

G — D — sim.

say you are a snuff queen. Hon-ey, I don't think that's true. So

G — A — 1. D

why don't we get drunk and screw? *Spoken: "Pick it coral reefers. Here we go."*

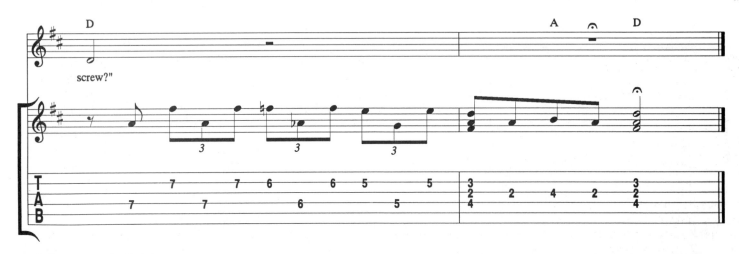

2. D

screw? Yeah now, ba - by, I said, "Why don't we get drunk and

D — A — D

screw?"

GUITAR TAB GLOSSARY **

TABLATURE EXPLANATION

READING TABLATURE: Tablature illustrates the six strings of the guitar. Notes and chords are indicated by the placement of fret numbers on a given string(s).

String ⑥, 3rd *Fret*   String ① 12th *Fret*   A "C" Chord   C Chord Arpeggiated
String ③ 13th *Fret*

BENDING NOTES

HALF STEP: Play the note and bend string one half step.*

WHOLE STEP: Play the note and bend string one whole step.

WHOLE STEP AND A HALF: Play the note and bend string a whole step and a half.

TWO STEPS: Play the note and bend string two whole steps.

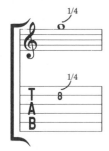

SLIGHT BEND (Microtone): Play the note and bend string slightly to the equivalent of half a fret.

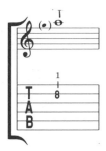

PREBEND (Ghost Bend): Bend to the specified note, before the string is picked.

PREBEND AND RELEASE: Bend the string, play it, then release to the original note.

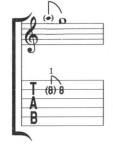

REVERSE BEND: Play the already-bent string, then immediately drop it down to the fretted note.

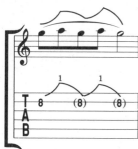

BEND AND RELEASE: Play the note and gradually bend to the next pitch, then release to the original note. Only the first note is attacked.

BENDS INVOLVING MORE THAN ONE STRING: Play the note and bend string while playing an additional note (or notes) on another string(s). Upon release, relieve pressure from additional note(s), causing original note to sound alone.

BENDS INVOLVING STATIONARY NOTES: Play notes and bend lower pitch, then hold until release begins (indicated at the point where line becomes solid).

UNISON BEND: Play both notes and immediately bend the lower note to the same pitch as the higher note.

DOUBLE NOTE BEND: Play both notes and immediately bend both strings simultaneously.

*A half step is the smallest interval in Western music; it is equal to one fret. A whole step equals two frets.

RHYTHM SLASHES

STRUM INDICATIONS: Strum with indicated rhythm.

The chord voicings are found on the first page of the transcription underneath the song title.

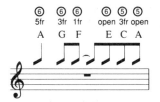

INDICATING SINGLE NOTES USING RHYTHM SLASHES: Very often single notes are incorporated into a rhythm part. The note name is indicated above the rhythm slash with a fret number and a string indication.

ARTICULATIONS

HAMMER ON: Play lower note, then "hammer on" to higher note with another finger. Only the first note is attacked.

LEFT HAND HAMMER: Hammer on the first note played on each string with the left hand.

PULL OFF: Play higher note, then "pull off" to lower note with another finger. Only the first note is attacked.

FRETBOARD TAPPING: "Tap" onto the note indicated by + with a finger of the pick hand, then pull off to the following note held by the fret hand.

TAP SLIDE: Same as fretboard tapping, but the tapped note is slid randomly up the fretboard, then pulled off to the following note.

BEND AND TAP TECHNIQUE: Play note and bend to specified interval. While holding bend, tap onto note indicated.

LEGATO SLIDE: Play note and slide to the following note. (Only first note is attacked).

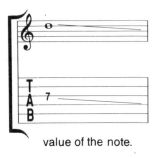

LONG GLISSANDO: Play note and slide in specified direction for the full value of the note.

SHORT GLISSANDO: Play note for its full value and slide in specified direction at the last possible moment.

PICK SLIDE: Slide the edge of the pick in specified direction across the length of the string(s).

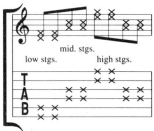

MUTED STRINGS: A percussive sound is made by laying the fret hand across all six strings while pick hand strikes specified area (low, mid, high strings).

PALM MUTE: The note or notes are muted by the palm of the pick hand by lightly touching the string(s) near the bridge.

TREMOLO PICKING: The note or notes are picked as fast as possible.

TRILL: Hammer on and pull off consecutively and as fast as possible between the original note and the grace note.

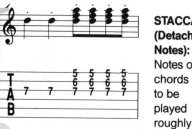

ACCENT: Notes or chords are to be played with added emphasis.

STACCATO (Detached Notes): Notes or chords are to be played roughly half their actual value and with separation.

DOWN STROKES AND UPSTROKES: Notes or chords are to be played with either a downstroke (⊓) or upstroke (∨) of the pick.

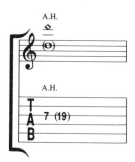

VIBRATO: The pitch of a note is varied by a rapid shaking of the fret hand finger, wrist, and forearm.

HARMONICS

NATURAL HARMONIC: A finger of the fret hand lightly touches the note or notes indicated in the tab and is played by the pick hand.

ARTIFICIAL HARMONIC: The first tab number is fretted, then the pick hand produces the harmonic by using a finger to lightly touch the same string at the second tab number (in parenthesis) and is then picked by another finger.

ARTIFICIAL "PINCH" HAR-MONIC: A note is fretted as indicated by the tab, then the pick hand produces the harmonic by squeezing the pick firmly while using the tip of the index finger in the pick attack. If parenthesis are found around the fretted note, it does not sound. No parenthesis means both the fretted note and A.H. are heard simultaneously.

TREMOLO BAR

SPECIFIED INTERVAL: The pitch of a note or chord is lowered to a specified interval and then may or may not return to the original pitch. The activity of the tremolo bar is graphically represented by peaks and valleys.

UN-SPECIFIED INTERVAL: The pitch of a note or a chord is lowered to an unspecified interval.